Rookie
Read-About Science®

It Could Still Be a Robot

By Allan Fowler

Consultants

Linda Cornwell, Learning Resource Consultant,
Indiana Department of Education

Fay Robinson, Child Development Specialist

Children's Press®
A Division of Grolier Publishing
New York   London   Hong Kong   Sydney
Danbury, Connecticut

Project Editor: Downing Publishing Services
Designer: Herman Adler Design Group
Photo Researcher: Caroline Anderson

Library of Congress Cataloging-in-Publication Data

Fowler, Allan.
    It could still be a robot / by Allan Fowler.
      p. cm. – (Rookie read-about science)
    Includes index.
    Summary: A simple introduction to smart machines, most of which currently
do not take human form, performing tasks too dangerous, too boring, or too
difficult for people to do.
    ISBN 0-516-20431-9 (lib. bdg)   0-516-26258-0 (pbk)
    1. Robots—Juvenile literature. [l. Automata.] I. Title. II. Series
TJ211.2.D68   1997   96-46949
629.8.'92–dc21   CIP
                                      AC

It's shaped like a person. It walks like a person. It talks like a person and makes choices like a person. It seems to be alive. Is it a real person?

No, it's a robot, made in
a factory — and covered
with metal instead of skin.

You might have seen
robots like these in
movies or TV shows
about the future or about
life on other worlds.

Maybe someday, a long time from now, there will be androids — robots that look and act like real people.

Not yet, though. Most of the robots we have today don't look anything like people.

A robot could be an arm without a body . . .

or just a box . . . and still
be a robot. Robots aren't
alive — since a robot is a
machine. A robot is a
"smart" machine.

Robots can do many of
the things that people do,
and some things people
can't do.

But each robot is built
to do only one thing or
certain types of things.

Robots often do jobs
that are unsafe for people
to do.

Factories use robots to pour hot metal.

Your family's car was probably spray painted by a robot, because paint fumes are bad for people's health.

Robot hands pick up
things that are dangerous
for people to touch.

Robots are used for tasks that would be boring or tiring for people.

Robots never get bored or tired.

They also do certain jobs better or faster than human beings can do them.

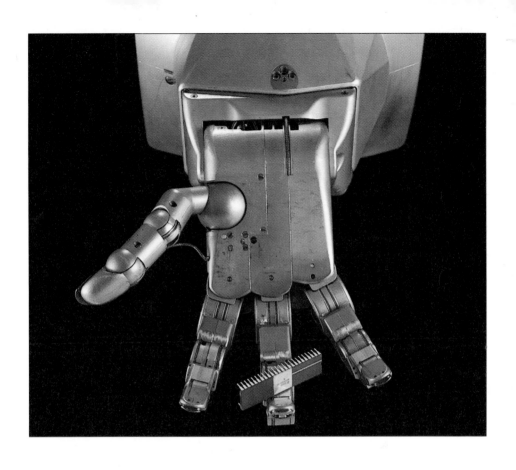

No person can handle very
tiny objects as easily as these
robot fingers can.

Some robots
help people
do things
they cannot
do for
themselves.

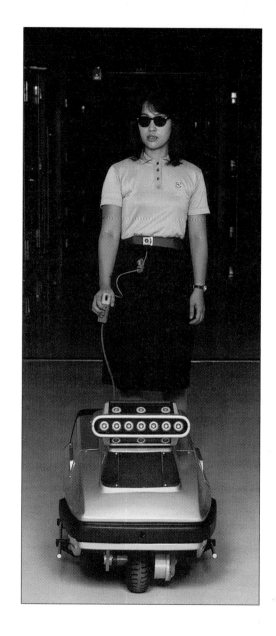

Some robots move
around. A robot might
roll on wheels . . .

or travel under water . . .

or even fly like this
robot plane that has no
human pilot . . . and still
be a robot.

But you won't often see a robot walking on two legs.

That's easy for you but hard for a robot.

Robots can go places where human beings can't go, such as the ocean bottom or the planet Mars.

21

At the end of a robot arm, there might be a hand with fingers . . . or a claw . . . or some kind of tool. It depends on what work the robot was built to do.

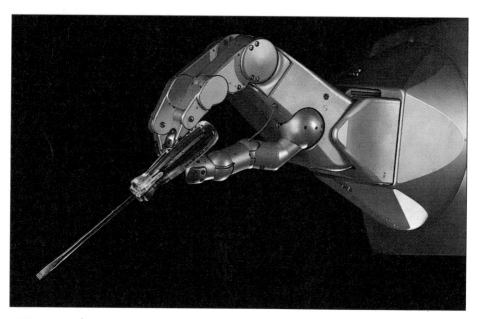

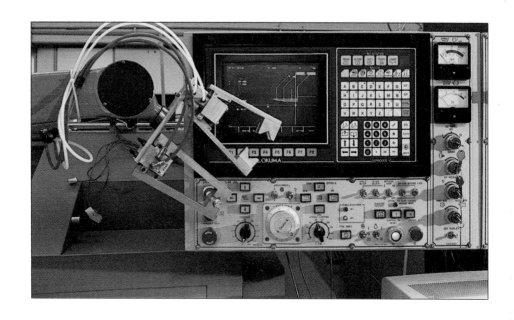

Robots today are run by computers. If its computer program is changed, a robot might be able to change from one type of job to another.

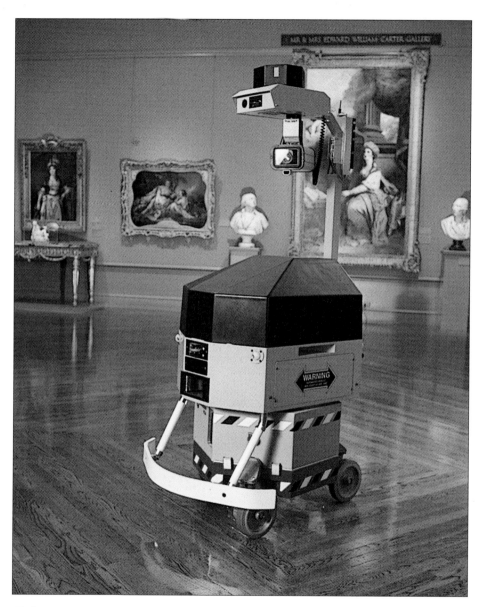

This rolling robot has an electronic "eye," like a camcorder or a TV remote control.

The "eye" can tell if something is blocking the robot's path.

Then the robot can move around whatever is in its way.

Other robots are guided
by sound or touch. So a
robot could be said to see,
hear, or feel . . . and still
be a robot.

A robot might be keeping
your school building from
getting too warm or too
cold. A robot might open
doors for people . . . solve
hard math problems . . .

draw pictures . . .

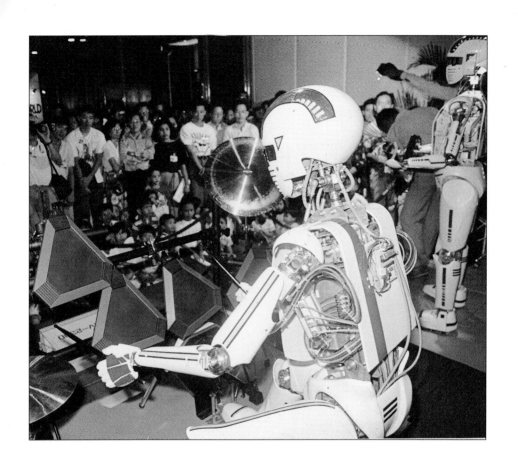

play a musical instrument . . .
or spin tops . . . and still be
a robot.

But it can't feel great or feel bad . . . enjoy a joke, a story, or a song . . . taste food . . . or love someone. Only human beings can do those things.

Words You Know

android

robot

factory

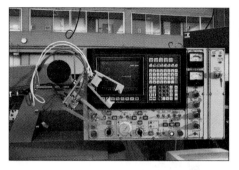
computer

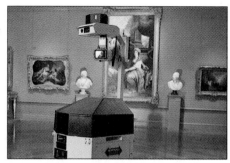
electronic eye

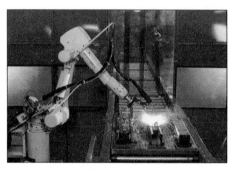
robot arm

robot claw

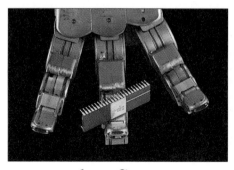
robot fingers

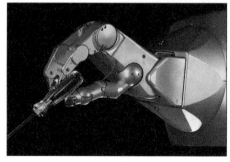
robot hand

Index

About the Author

Allan Fowler is a free-lance writer with a background in advertising.
Born in New York, he lives in Chicago now and enjoys traveling.

Photo Credits

Thiis colorful, fact-f
Science book describ
smart machines—most of which currently do not take
human form—that perform tasks too dangerous, too
boring, or too difficult for people to do.

Read these other Rookie Read-About® Science books:

- Feeling Things
- Hot and Cold
- Mirror, Mirror
- Recycle That!

- Seeing Things
- Solid, Liquid, or Gas
- Too Much Trash!
- What Magnets Can Do

CHILDREN'S PRESS

U.S. $4.95
Can. $6.95

ISBN 0-516-26258-0

9 780516 262581

90000>